LaDonna C. Osborn

I0102004

Give Thanks

OSBORN
Ministries
International

USA HQ:

OSBORN MINISTRIES, INT'L

P.O. Box 10, Tulsa, OK 74102 USA

T.L. & DAISY OSBORN, CO-FOUNDERS
LADONNA C. OSBORN, CEO

Tel: 918/743-6231
Fax: 918/749-0339
E-Mail: ministry@osborn.org
www.osborn.org

Canada: Box 281 STN ADELAIDE, Toronto ON M5C 2J4
England: Box 148, Birmingham B3 2LG
(A Registered Charity)

iii

ISBN 978-0-87943-193-8
Copyright 2012 by LaDonna C. Osborn
Printed in USA 2012-10
All Rights Reserved

CONTENTS

DEDICATED

This book is dedicated to every believer in Jesus Christ who has discovered and embraced the marvelous truths of His redeeming work, who eagerly shares His Good News with others and who lives each day in awed gratitude for His amazing love, grace and presence.

Dr. LaDonna C. Osborn

Foreword

IT IS WONDERFUL to be part of Christ's Body, His Church. We are a community of faith. And as such, we offer a message that is different from what empty religions offer. Our message is:

- One of hope,
- One of purpose and
- One of miracles.

We do not have to succumb to the problems that life brings. We are a community that embodies the divine heart of God that is bigger than any human problem.

This *Sermon-in-Print* message will stir your heart toward the God to whom we should GIVE THANKS. Inspired by Psalm 100, the truths contained in this pocketbook will cause you to discover the greatness of your redeemed status in Jesus Christ. The God who provides redemption through Jesus is the God who loves you, who cares for you, who is faithful to you and who never leaves you. His redemption of you is at work every day, in every situation.

We have profound reasons to GIVE THANKS.

LaDonna C. Osborn, D.Min.

✳

PSALMS 100

SHOUT FOR JOY to the Lord, all the earth.
  Worship the Lord with gladness;
  come before him with joyful songs.
Know that the Lord is God.
  It is he who made us, and we are his;
  we are his people, the sheep of his pasture.

Enter his gates with thanksgiving
  and his courts with praise;
  give thanks to him and praise his name.
For the Lord is good and his love endures
    forever;
  his faithfulness continues through all
    generations.

Chapter 1

12 Reasons to GIVE THANKS

IN THE UNITED STATES we celebrate a holiday known as Thanksgiving. It is a day for remembering how blessed we are as Americans. Although it is not a Christian holiday as is Christmas or Easter, Thanksgiving is a day that focuses our thoughts on God, who is the giver of every good gift. It is a time of lifting up our voices in gratefulness and appreciation, of remembering the positive aspects of our country's history and of re-affirming that we were founded as a God-honoring nation.

Likewise, around the world Christians of many nations and all traditions gather at various times to convene "Thanksgiving Services" where believers are encouraged to express their gratitude to the Lord, according to the Scripture, for His bountiful blessings.

Give praise to the Lord, call on his name; make known among the nations what he has done. Sing of him, sing his praises; tell of all his wonderful acts. Remember the wonders he has done, his miracles... He is the Lord our God... Psa.105:1-2,5,7

We strive to express through our lives each day the same spirit of gratitude that is demonstrated in our homes and churches during those specific times of thanksgiving.

We who are Christian believers have a particular and profound reason to be thankful:

> # Through JESUS CHRIST, we have been redeemed.

Psalm 100 is a beautiful declaration of the goodness of God who has provided complete redemption for us through Jesus Christ. This psalm reveals to us a pattern of how we can offer our thanksgiving to Him:

Shout for joy to the Lord, all the earth.
  Worship the Lord with gladness;
  come before him with joyful songs.
Know that the Lord is God.
  It is he who made us, and we are his;
  we are his people, the sheep of his pasture.

Enter his gates with thanksgiving and
  his courts with praise;
  give thanks to him and praise his name.
For the Lord is good and his love endures
  forever;
  his faithfulness continues through all
  generations.[Psa.100:1-5]

While meditating on this psalm and considering the greatness of God's love toward people, I began to ponder the word *thanksgiving*.

1. What exactly does it mean to have a spirit of thanksgiving?

2. How can we better understand what thanksgiving truly is and why we must maintain a thankful heart?

In answer to these questions, the Lord inspired me with an acronym of the word *thanksgiving*.

✧✧✧

T – TRANSGRESSIONS REMITTED

As followers of Jesus Christ, we GIVE THANKS because:

> — *Our transgressions*
> *–our sins–*
> *are removed.* —

Jesus' blood was shed for the remission of sin.

For this is My blood of the new covenant, which is shed for many for the remission of sins.^{Mat.26:28 NKJV} *And where these have been forgiven, sacrifice for sin is no longer necessary.*^{Heb.10:18}

- Remission of sin is a complete release from the guilt or penalty of past sin, and a total restoration to our former status and condition before sin entered.

- Remission of sin involves a payment in full, as if the debt is no longer owed.

Therefore, remission of sins means that our transgressions or evil deeds are completely wiped away, that the slate of our past is clean and that our sins are no longer remembered.

... *"Their sins and lawless acts I will remember no more."* [Heb.10:17] *as far as the east is from the west, so far has he removed our transgressions from us.* [Psa.103:12]

**GOD'S REMISSION OF OUR SINS
is much greater than
His forgiveness only.**

In the Old Testament, the people of God

were forgiven when the priest made atonement for their sins through the sacrifice of bulls, goats or some other animal. These blood sacrifices yielded a temporary forgiveness or atonement (covering) that had to be repeated regularly to atone for any newly committed sins.

The law is only a shadow of the good things that are coming — not the realities themselves. For this reason it can never, by the same sacrifices repeated endlessly year after year, make perfect those who draw near to worship. Otherwise, would they not have stopped being offered? For the worshipers would have been cleansed once for all, and would no longer have felt guilty for their sins. But those sacrifices are an annual reminder of sins. It is impossible for the blood of bulls and goats to take away sins.[Heb.10:1-4]

We, the redeemed, are thankful because the shed blood of Jesus Christ has remitted our transgressions, once and for all.

*First he said, "Sacrifices and offerings, burnt offerings and sin offerings you did not desire…Here I am, I have come to do your will." He sets aside the first to establish the second. And by that will, we have been made holy through the sacrifice of the body of Jesus Christ once for all. For by one sacrifice he has made perfect forever those who are being made holy.*Heb.10:9-10,12,14

Our past iniquities plus the separation from God that we endured because of our sins, have been removed…obliterated. We are thankful to the Lord for thoroughly removing our transgressions. No other sacrifice will ever be needed. Jesus paid the entire price for us to be restored to Him, free from guilt and condemnation.

*…We have peace with God through our Lord Jesus Christ.*Rom.5:1

Because our sins have been removed, we are restored to full relationship with God.

This is redemption.

We have been bought back by our Creator through His action on the cross on our behalf.

But we must remember that being redeemed does not simply mean that we are part of a "sign your name and you're a member" society. When we believe on Christ and receive His divine life, we are redeemed (bought back), and His life takes over. Our old lives are gone and a new life has begun.

Therefore, if anyone is in Christ, the new creation has come: The old has gone, the new is here! 2Cor.5:17

The essence of being a Christian is that the life of Jesus is now expressed through the born again believer. Our lives become an expression of our faith in Him and His lifestyle displays His presence in us. This is the boundless truth of redemption at work through each believer:

> **A PERSON FREED**
> from the bondage of sin.
>
> **A PERSON EXPRESSING**
> the life of Christ to others.

Therefore, in looking at the acronym for *thanksgiving*, we do not simply create a ritualistic checklist of things for which to be thankful. Yes, our sins are forgiven and blotted out, but we also remember that we are now free to live with a new quality of peace because our sins are remitted.

You see, how you live each day is the indication of what you know about Christ's sacrifice for you and the provisions that are yours through Him. God's desire is that you live as though your sins are remitted.

So then, just as you received Christ Jesus

*as Lord, continue to live your lives in him, rooted and built up in him, strengthened in the faith as you were taught, and overflowing with thankfulness.*Col.2:6-7

The devil wants to restrict redeemed believers from truly living their redeemed lifestyle. He is a thief and a liar, a deceiver and a destroyer. Remain alert, because the enemy has countless ways of suggesting that your transgressions still remain. His lies threaten to be a mystical cloud of influence that pulls on you, causing you to do things that you do not want to do and to think things that are not true.

Recognize this enemy of your soul and resist him. Then you can begin to walk in the wonderful freedom of Christ who has come to live His life through you.

When you were dead in your sins and in the uncircumcision of your sinful nature, God made you alive with Christ. He forgave us all our sins, having canceled the charge of our legal indebtedness, which stood against us and condemned us; he has taken it away, nailing it to the cross.^{Col.2:13-14}

✧✧✧

SO WE ARE thankful because our transgressions have been remitted.

1. We are born again.
2. We are forgiven.
3. We are new.
4. The old is passed.
5. Yesterday's mistakes and sins are no longer relevant.

How far is east from west? Too far to measure. Our sins are gone for eternity. Our past transgressions are forever blotted out!

We now walk in newness of life and GIVE THANKS because *our transgressions have been remitted.*

✧✧✧

H – HEALTH RENEWED

As followers of Christ we GIVE THANKS, because:

— Our health is renewed. —

We have been healed by the stripes and wounds of Jesus. He paid the tremendous price, at the cross, to reverse the consequences of our sin.

So the questions that follow are:

Are we healthy?

Are we walking in the provision that Christ extends to us?

But he was pierced for our transgressions, he was crushed for our iniquities; the punishment that brought us peace was upon him, and by his wounds we are healed.[Isa.53:5]

So, when were we healed?

When Christ suffered on our behalf.

If we are not walking in health, then this is the day to begin a new lifestyle of faith and thanksgiving for God's provision of wholeness. Isaiah 53:5 and many other Bible passages are firm reminders that our health is renewed through Jesus Christ. We thank God for that endowment.

...I am the LORD, who heals you." Ex 15:26

...I am the Lord, the God of the whole human race. Is anything too hard for me? Jer 32:26-27

He sent out his word and healed them; he rescued them from the grave. Psa 107:20

Praise the Lord, my soul, and forget not all his benefits — who forgives all your sins and heals all your diseases, Psa.103:2-3

We can stand steadfastly on God's Word of promise, or we can choose to negate

God's supernatural provisions based on natural circumstances. Many influences around us contradict the reality of the Word of God.

For example, the secular assumption is that when we reach a certain age, things happen to cause our bodies to break down and stop functioning. We are told that it's *normal* to have pain; if we live to be a certain age we can expect inevitable physical ailments.

The redeemed man or woman must decide whether they will believe those negative assumptions or whether they will live by faith in the Word of God.

As believers, we are challenged to trust the Word of God above all other facts. Remember, we are healed by Jesus' stripes. That is the truth. As children of God we have been *"called...out of **darkness** into **His wonderful light**."*[1Pet.2:9] Although we live in a world that is corrupted by sin, we are called to live according to the Good News of Christ's redemption triumph. We are *in* the world, but we are not *of* the world. We have been born (again) from above.

This miracle reality becomes our divine lifestyle when we KNOW what Christ has provided and when we BELIEVE that we are personally included in His action.

Jesus refers to us in His prayer: *They are not of the world, even as I am not of it.*[Jn.17:16] *But to all who received (Jesus), who believed in his name, he gave power to become children of God, who were born, not of blood or of the will of the flesh or of the will of man, but of God.*[Jn.1:12-13 NRSV]

❖❖❖

SO WE LIFT our hearts and GIVE THANKS to God, knowing that everything—which was once wrong in our lives because of sin—is now made right. **Because of the cross of our Lord Jesus Christ,** *our health is renewed.*

✧✧✧

A – AUTHORITY REGAINED

As believers we GIVE THANKS because we are not victims.

— We have authority. —

To understand this authority we must review God's original plan for His human family. In that inceptive plan, people were given responsibility and authority as custodians over all of God's creation. God created a man and formed a woman and gave them instructions to rule the earth.

Then God said, "Let us make human beings in our image, in our likeness, so that they may rule over the fish in the sea and the birds in the sky, over the livestock and all the wild animals and over all the creatures that move along the ground (emphasis added)." Gen.1:26

So we see that in God's initial plan, people were entrusted with authority to rule all that He had created.

Then Satan–the deceiver–entered the scene with his corrupt plan. (Genesis 3) Adam and Eve chose to distrust God and His Word, believing the lies of Satan. Doubting God and His Word was the sin of Adam and Eve that led to their rebellion against God and their willful disobedience of His instruction to not eat from the tree of the knowledge of good and evil.

When Adam and Eve willfully turned away from their Creator and His beautiful plan, they became slaves of sin and death. Satan became their ruler. This was not God's design for His beloved human creation. Each person born into the world–from that time until now–is born into the consequences of Adam and Eve's transgression. Thus, all people living who have not been redeemed by the blood of Jesus Christ, are living in bondage to Satan.

God's beautiful blueprint, for His image-and-likeness creation to live under His love-reign, became corrupted and all human persons became slaves under the death-reign of Satan.

But when God came to earth in the flesh of Jesus Christ, to be the redeeming sacrifice for humankind:

- He paid the full penalty for our sin;

- He defeated the enemy who had seized the power over us; and

- He destroyed the works of death that had infected the human family.

Since the children have flesh and blood, he too shared in their humanity so that by his death he might break the power of him who holds the power of death — that is, the devil — and free those who all their lives were held in slavery by their fear of death.[Heb.2:14-15]

The reason the Son of God appeared was to destroy the devil's work.[1Jn.3:8b]

Through the redemptive work of Jesus Christ, God returned to people–those who believe on Him–the authority that they had in the beginning. This is an amazing truth.

(Jesus said) *I will give **you** the keys of the kingdom of heaven; whatever **you** bind* (or do not permit) *on earth will be bound in heaven, and whatever **you** loose* (or permit) *on earth will be loosed in heaven* (emphases added).[Mat.16:19]

(Again Jesus said) *I have given **you** authority to trample on snakes and scorpions*

and to overcome all the power of the enemy;
nothing will harm you (emphases added).
Lu.10:19

It is essential for us to realize that, through Christ, we have power over the adversary!

The questions we must ask ourselves are:

1. Are we using the power and authority that God ordained for us as His creation?

2. Are we overcomers in every situation, or are we merely victims of our circumstances?

Review your own attitude toward life's circumstances.

- Do you feel used by others?

- Do you believe that your life is insignificant?

- Do you anticipate with dread that certain things may happen to you?

- Do you feel helpless against life's situations?

- Do you feel that your only option is to just cope with your circumstances?

- Do you fear the devil and his evil schemes?

As you consider what it means to have a heart of thankfulness, remember that Christ regained your authority for you and you are now more than a conqueror in Him if you chose to believe His Word and begin exercising that power.

...in all these things we are more than conquerors through him who loved us.[Rom.8:37]

I can do all this through him who gives me strength.[Phil.4:13]

Jesus' earthly life is our example of

how we are to live with supernatural authority. Jesus did not base His actions on the world's conclusions, but on what His heavenly Father told Him. In the same way:

> **We must live our lives based on the authority of our heavenly Father's Word.**

Jesus did not respond to conditions according to the social or religious norms of His day.

> **Jesus knew who He was and on every occasion He functioned in the reality of His identity in the Father.**

Likewise, we are to discover our new

identity in Christ and act accordingly without fear.

...If God is for us, who can be against us? Rom.8:31

for it is God who works in you to will and to act in order to fulfill his good purpose. Phil.2:13

Believe in the Christ who comes to live in you.

Believe in His ultimate authority and in His good will toward you.

Believe that He is on your side as you allow Him to express His love and life through you.

What happens when we live in our redemptive power and authority?

We are victorious over the enemy.

We walk with confidence.

We bring peace to troubled circumstances.

We respond in gentleness rather than reacting in anger.

We do not succumb to life's pressures but we speak the life-giving Word of God in all situations.

We forgive others.

We never give up.

We know who we are and what we have.

Remember that Jesus said, *I have given you authority to trample on snakes and scorpions and to overcome all the power of the enemy; nothing will harm you.*[Lu.10:19]

❖❖❖

JESUS GAVE HIS disciples—He gives to us—authority to overcome all the obstacles of the enemy. **This is a great reason to GIVE THANKS. We have *regained our authority.***

❖❖❖

N – NAME RECORDED

Jesus Christ is referred to in Scripture as the Sacrificial Lamb of God. As redeemed believers we GIVE THANKS because Christ's sacrifice for us has made it possible for,

> *– our names to be recorded –*
> in the Lamb's Book of Life.

I did not see a temple in the city, because the Lord God Almighty and the Lamb are its temple. The city does not need the sun or the moon to shine on it, for the glory of God gives it light, and the Lamb is its lamp. The nations will walk by its light, and the kings of the earth will bring their splendor into it. On no day will its gates ever be shut, for there will be no night there. The glory and honor of the nations will be brought into it. Nothing impure will ever enter it, (the New

Jerusalem) *nor will anyone who does what is shameful or deceitful, but only those whose names are written in* **the Lamb's book of life** (emphasis added).[Rev.21:22-27]

We learn from this that God takes decisive action to include the individual name of each person who believes in what Christ did at the cross on his or her behalf. This is an overwhelming biblical fact that we accept by faith. Our names are recorded in this book of LIFE because of the Lamb of God.

What do you think about when you think of the Lamb?

1. I think about *sacrifice*.

2. I think about *blood*.

3. I think about *suffering*.

4. I think about *innocence*.

5. I think about *finality*.

6. I think about the *divine miracle of love*.

7. I think and remember that *only Jesus has the power to include our names in is Book of Life*.

The Lamb, Christ Jesus–with His own blood–earned the right to include our names in His Book of Life. He does this for *everyone who believes*. The Lamb is the one who guarantees your entry in His book. No one else can do that.

I see the grace of God in Jesus Christ as He stands guard over the Book of Life so that the enemy cannot erase even one name among those who belong to God.

(Jesus said) *While I was with them, I protected them and kept them safe by that name you gave me. None has been lost except the one doomed to destruction so that Scripture would be fulfilled.*[Jn.17:12]

If Jesus kept all of those who were

given to Him (except for Judas), then He is certainly able to keep you.

The Scripture assures us that Jesus loved all His disciples...and He loved them until the end. *It was just before the Passover Festival. Jesus knew that the hour had come for him to leave this world and go to the Father. Having loved his own who were in the world, he loved them to the end.* Jn.13:1

As we continue to ponder the many reasons that we are thankful, let us rejoice in the fact that our *names* were recorded in the Lamb's Book of Life the moment that we believed in and accepted Jesus Christ as Savior and Lord. Remember that God knows *your* name. Be confident that He has included *your* name in His eternal book that is sealed with the blood of Christ.

So, of course, the important question is:

Are you living as though your name is recorded in Christ's eternal book?

When our names are included in God's record, every area of our lives becomes new. This new status becomes the reality that changes everything in our lives on earth.

✧✧✧

Do NOT BE limited by what the systems of the world say about you.

You are redeemed.

You are loved by God.

You are not a stranger to God.

You are God's child.

Your Heavenly Father knows your name.

He has written YOU into His book.

GIVE THANKS

We GIVE THANKS to Jesus Christ, the Sacrificial Lamb of God, because *our names are recorded* in the Lamb's Book of Life.

❖❖❖

K – KINSHIP RESTORED

We GIVE THANKS because through Jesus Christ,

> —*our kinship relationship*
> *with God is restored.*—

This means that we are now of the same lineage as God. He is our Heavenly Father. We are from the same family as Jesus Christ. We are kinfolk with God Himself. We also share a spiritual relationship with the entire community of the redeemed, with the saints of old and with everyone who has received Jesus Christ and His eternal life.

The Apostle John says it so clearly: *Yet to all who did receive him* (Jesus), *to those who believed in his name, he gave the right to become children of God...*(emphasis added) Jn.1:12

You and I are among those who have received Jesus. He has given to you and me the right to be His kinfolk, His children and relatives within His family. That is an authentic reason to be thankful.

Just think of it:

We are not spiritually homeless.

We are not spiritual wanderers.

We are not nameless or forgotten orphans.

We are no longer separated from God.

We are not without identity.

We are esteemed as royal kinfolk of the God of creation.

Jesus Christ has reconnected us to our eternal Father and has established us in our rightful inheritance.

Allow me to ask some piercing questions.

1. In the privacy of your life, do you ever lament familial, biological relationships?

2. Do you experience emotional pain because of your parents or because of your children?

3. Have any of your relatives said or done things that bruised you physically or emotionally?

4. Do you ever suffer in some area because of your natural family?

If so, I encourage you to allow the Holy Spirit of God to rise within you and to heal the wounds that you have suffered.

Allow the Lord to reaffirm your intimate kinship with God as your Father.

He loves you and He has the power to heal what is bruised or broken. The blood of Christ now covers all the disappointments and suffering that you have endured through natural family relationships. You can put those issues in God's hands and trust Him to take care of them.

You cannot change other people.

You cannot go back in time and undo yesterday's events.

But you can turn your face to the One who calls you His kin. He steps in to shield you and to heal you because He loves you. You are His child. It is your right to be in His family and to experience the same benefits that every other member of His family enjoys.

❖❖❖

ALLOW YOUR KINSHIP connection with God, through Jesus, to be the healing reality in your life.

• Meditate on your status as God's child.

• Allow His truth to permeate your thinking and your emotions.

• Let the oil of God's healing presence turn your mourning into rejoicing.

You now belong to the entire family of God, so GIVE THANKS to Him for accepting you as His child. *Your kinship with God has been restored.*

✧✧✧

S – SONG RETURNED

We can GIVE THANKS to our loving Redeemer because:

—our song has returned.—

He put a new song in my mouth, a hymn of praise to our God…^{Psa.40:3}

When Jesus saves us, we are once again capable of singing a new song to the Lord. It is a song of praise and gratitude, not a song of lament or defeat. It is a song of resurrection, not a song of death.

1. It is a song of joy and freedom.

2. It is a song of grace and mercy.

3. It is a song of acceptance and relationship.

4. It is a song of love and purpose.

5. It is a song of forgiveness and new beginnings.

6. It is a song of gratitude and worship.

7. It is a song of devotion and allegiance.

Think of it! We are singers. Some of us may not have beautiful voices, but we are all redeemed singers with a beautiful melody of praise to our Redeemer in our hearts and on our lips.

I love to hear children sing. A child's song is pure. There is no embarrassment or pride to mask the song. A child can just sing with his or her whole heart even if no one is listening.

When I hear a child sing with that level of abandon, I realize that *a song is our natural expression of the joy that God puts in our hearts*. It is wonderful that God gave us voices to make melody, with rhythm and harmony, to make a beautiful sound of gratitude to our God.

Our song was once distorted and misdirected by sin. But God intended that our song be for Him. Now that we are redeemed, our joyful song has returned. Our song is no longer a sad, lonely ballad. Our song is now a song of praise and rejoicing. It is a song of joy and of thanksgiving. It is a song that declares the greatness of God and echoes His glorious works.

When we gather with other believers at our home church, *International Gospel Center*, we lift our voices in praise and worship through singing. One of my favorite songs expresses with profound simplicity the reason for our song.

When I Think About The Lord

When I think about the Lord
How He saved me
How He raised me
How He filled me up with the Holy Ghost
How He healed me to the uttermost

When I think about the Lord
How He picked me up and turned me around
And set my feet on solid ground

It makes me want to shout
Hallelujah
Thank You Jesus
Lord You're worthy of all the glory
All the honor
All the praises

When I Think About The Lord
by: James Huey (at age 14)
© 1998 CFN Music

❖❖❖

WHAT CHRIST HAS done for us is great. That is why we are filled with thanks. We are redeemed. Christ Himself has returned our song and now we sing.

No matter the quality of our natural voices, **let us daily raise them to GIVE THANKS to the One who has** *returned to us our song.*

❖❖❖

G – GUILT REMOVED

We consider the amazing power of Christ's redemptive work and we GIVE THANKS because He has:

—*removed all guilt from our lives.*—

For us to grasp this profound truth, we must first recognize the difference between *transgression* and *guilt*.

> **A transgression is the *fact*.**
> **Guilt is the *feeling*.**

We have previously considered how Jesus has remitted (removed) our transgressions (or sins). That is a redemption fact. But often, Christians find it difficult to release the guilt that accompanies the memory of their past sins.

Why? Because the enemy of the cross (the devil himself) is the deceiver and liar who cunningly reminds believers of their past sins. Satan comes to infiltrate our thoughts through accusations that produce guilt and condemnation.

Then I heard a loud voice in heaven say:

> *"Now have come the salvation*
> *and the power*
> > *and the kingdom of our God,*
> > *and the authority of his*
> *Messiah.*
> *For the accuser of our brothers*
> *and sisters,*
> > *who accuses them before our*
> *God day and night,*
> > *has been hurled down.*Rev.12:10

The enemy drags around the debris and garbage of our old lives, ignoring the reality that Jesus has assumed our sins in His own body. The accuser tries to reposition that guilt back on us.

It is vital that believers understand that the devil is eternally evil. Remember, he is a liar and the truth is not in him. It grieves me to see how many Christians have been tricked by the enemy causing them to live with guilt over some area of their past lives.

...the devil...was a murderer from the beginning, not holding to the truth, for there is no truth in him. When he lies, he speaks his native language, for he is a liar and the father of lies.[Jn.8:44]

According to the Scripture, we are empowered to resist the devil through faith in what Christ has accomplished for us.

Submit yourselves, then, to God. Resist the devil, and he will flee from you.[Jas.4:7]

As believers we can choose to resist feelings of guilt, by remembering the grace of God that provided this great salvation.

During one of my international *Gospel Seminars* for Christians, pastors and church leaders, I was teaching those who had gathered from various nations. I ministered to the leaders for three sessions. During the fourth session, I felt impressed to preach about the cross of Christ and to give them an opportunity to accept Christ.

It was deeply moving to see many church leaders and pastors coming forward weeping, admitting that they had never understood salvation and had never accepted Christ personally.

It was unlikely that all of those who came forward were unconverted. Yet this illustrates how many precious believers in Christ endure a lingering sense of guilt, causing them to be uncertain of their own relationship with God.

Guilt is debilitating.

Guilt is mental bondage.

Guilt denies the effectiveness of the work of Christ at the cross.

Guilt is the attempt of the devil to sabotage the joy and peace that belongs to every born again child of God.

Guilt prevents many Christians from being effective witnesses of Christ among their friends and associates.

*...there is **now** no condemnation for those who are in Christ Jesus,* (emphasis added) Rom.8:1

✧✧✧

THIS IS A great reason to GIVE THANKS.
From the time we accepted Jesus Christ,
we have been delivered from the guilt
of our past sins. We now accept by faith
that what Jesus did at the cross was
sufficient to deal with all of our transgressions.

We **accept** it.

We **trust** in the Lord Jesus.

Our guilt has been removed.

❖❖❖

I – INFERIORITY REPLACED

We GIVE THANKS because of what Jesus endured on our behalf, our,

—inferiority is replaced—
by a deep inner, godly confidence.

A new consciousness begins to develop in the psyche — in the mind and heart — of the redeemed man or woman.

The Apostle Peter describes this new status in Christ.

But you are a chosen people, a royal priesthood, a holy nation, God's special possession... 1Pet.2:9a

We are to see ourselves from this redeemed perspective:

We are *chosen*.

We are *royal*.

We are *special*.

We are *accepted*.

We have *purpose*.

...that you may declare the praises of him who called you out of darkness into his wonderful light. Once you were not a people, but now you are the people of God; once you had not received mercy, but now you have received mercy.[1Pet.2:9b-10]

We are *called*.

We are the *people of God*.

We have *received His mercy*.

Before Christ, we were wanderers. We were lost. Our pasts were cluttered with misdeeds. Our futures were haunted by fears and condemnation. But Jesus stood up in the midst of our disgrace and said, "You are chosen. You are special. You are redeemed."

You did not choose me, but I chose you and appointed you so that you might go and bear fruit...[Jn.15:16]

Most of us experience inferiority in some area of our lives. Inferiority is the feeling of inadequacy that makes us think that we are lacking, especially when we compare ourselves to others. Inferiority suggests that we have a subordinate status, that we are deficient or weak or mediocre.

What causes feelings of inferiority?

The root of all inferiority is sin — separation from God and His divine life.

People were not created to feel inferior. When sin entered the human family, the sense of inferiority etched itself onto the psyche of humanity, and that mark is deep and universal. Some people project an image of self-importance. However, this is usually a cover up for their deeper feelings of inadequacy and mediocrity.

Men and women without Christ do not feel good about themselves. They do not feel special. Often even those who achieve a measure of success, feel that they are living as frauds, because their outward success does not reflect what they feel internally. So, many people live continually trying to prove themselves...trying to measure up or to be good enough.

If you have accepted Jesus into your life but you continue to live with a sense of inferiority, it is time for you to accept your new status in Christ. Remind yourself, "I am special; I am chosen. I am elite in Christ."

For you are a people holy to the LORD your God. The LORD your God has chosen you out of all the peoples on the face of the earth to be his people, his treasured pos-

session…because the LORD loved you and kept the oath he swore…he brought you out with a mighty hand and redeemed you…
Deut.7:6,8

No one can take that faith-stand for you. When the enemy comes to you with accusing taunts, reminding you of your inferiority, repeat to him who you are in Christ. Reject his lies. Believe what God has said about you in His Word.

✧✧✧

TO LIVE FREE of inferiority is a discipline of faith in Christ who has redeemed you to a royal, priestly heritage. **As you exercise faith in that redemption truth, you will walk free from bondage because your *inferiority has been replaced* with godly dignity! Therefore, GIVE THANKS to Jesus Christ, your Redeemer.**

✧✧✧

V – VALUE RESTATED

Another reason that we GIVE THANKS to God is because:

— *Our value is restated.* —

Notice that I did not say that our value is *reinstated*. It has been *restated*. There is a difference.

1. If our value is *reinstated,* that would imply that there was a time when we had no value and Christ came so that we could become valuable again. No.

2. Our value is *restated,* which means that there was never a time when we were not valuable. God always treasured us. Christ came *because* we are valuable. He came and

restated the eternal fact of our worth.

The way that you think about yourself is totally revolutionized when you grasp this biblical concept. When you accept your true value, when you highly esteem your own life, you no longer live with a sense of inferiority.

what are human beings that you are mindful of them, mortals that you care for them? Yet you have made them a little lower than God, and crowned them with glory and honor. You have given them dominion over the works of your hands; you have put all things under their feet, Psa.8:4-6 NRSV

See what great love the Father has lavished on us, that we should be called children of God! And that is what we are! The reason the world does not know us is that it did not know him. 1Jn.3:1

Think about this: If a scientist were to

reduce you to the basic chemicals and elements of your physical body, what would you be worth? Perhaps not much. But when you discover your immeasurable, divine worth, you no longer allow temporal standards to measure your value. Because you understand the redemption truth of *value restated*, you no longer allow secular society to determine your worth. Material possessions do not establish your value. The opinions of others do not dictate your importance. Achievements add nothing to your true significance. Titles or social position do not define your infinite importance.

> **God Himself establishes your eternal worth.**

For you know that it was not with perishable things such as silver or gold that you were redeemed from the empty way of life handed down to you from your ancestors, but with the precious blood of Christ, a lamb without blemish or defect.[1Pet.1:18-19]

Can you imagine the value of the precious blood of Jesus Christ that He willingly exchanged for you? His blood was the most valuable gift of all time. *Thanks be to God for his indescribable gift!* 2Cor.9:15

❖❖❖

THIS BIBLICAL TRUTH influences how we face each day and every circumstance.

We are valued, so we can value others.

We are valued, so we can live with dignity and purpose.

We will forever GIVE THANKS for the redeeming work of Christ at the cross, because through Him, *our value is restated.*

❖❖❖

I - INSPIRATION REIGNITED

We GIVE THANKS because through the redemption in Christ, we are rescued from a life of drudgery and hopelessness and have been:

—Brought into a life of light and inspiration.—

People who have never experienced the redeeming power of Jesus inevitably wrestle with a heaviness of spirit that weighs them down.

Wherever I go in the world I see people who are weary, indifferent or despondent. Beggars on the street live with a sense of hopelessness. People in prisons or hospitals are often disheartened and oppressed. Others are at shopping malls, in city parks, at schools, in places of business or in homes, busy with life, yet there is no life in them. People without Christ are weary.

This look of lifelessness on people's faces and this lack of energy and enthusiasm in their actions are indications that they don't know Jesus. Without Him, people are dull and drab; they are tired and bored. Jesus is the one who ignites His inspiration deep within the human person.

Praise be to the God and Father of our Lord Jesus Christ! In his great mercy he has given us new birth into a living hope through the resurrection of Jesus Christ from the dead...In all this you greatly rejoice... though you have not seen him, you love him;...you believe in him and are filled with an inexpressible and glorious joy, for you are receiving...the salvation of your souls.[1Pet. 1:3,6,8,9]

And hope does not put us to shame, be-

cause God's love has been poured out into our hearts through the Holy Spirit, who has been given to us. Rom.5:5

Whether people are wealthy or poor, educated or illiterate, old or young, female or male, without that spark of divine inspiration from Christ that ignites their spirit, there can be no genuine inspiration in life.

Refuse to live as a Christian with a sense of weariness and defeat. Meditate on what Christ has accomplished for you through His redeeming work. I suggest that you visit our ministry website at *www.osborn.org*. There you have free access to all 52 of my lessons on Redemption, presented in four complete study courses. When you fully understand all that is included for you in God's action of redemption through Jesus Christ, your life will never the same.

Redemption truths ignite and inspire

your sense of excitement in life. The power of God's Spirit gives you energy that you have never experienced. Learning of Christ and His infinite provisions for you provide the zest for living that gives you a reason to get up each morning. His truths and His presence with you will put a spring in your step and help you to face life's circumstances with hope and confidence.

*May the God of hope fill you with all joy and peace as you trust in him, so that you may overflow with hope by the power of the Holy Spirit.*Rom.15:13

Think about what inspires you. I'm not referring to things like an increase in your salary, which most certainly would give a temporary sense of happiness. I am talking about that something that so inspires you that you can talk about it with a friend for hours. You're excited; you're inspired.

My friend, spending time in the presence of Jesus will genuinely inspire you on the deepest level! Just think of it. He's in you and wants to fill you up. *Out of his fullness we have all received...* [Jn.1:16] His presence is able to ignite you and energize you. Jesus wants you to be brimming with His life and energy.

When you are filled with Jesus, *filled with the fruit of righteousness that comes through Jesus Christ — to the glory and praise of God* [Phil.1:11] you will be different from those around you. Your presence among others will introduce a greater sense of joy and purpose. People will enjoy being around you because you are not burdened by the circumstances of life.

Jesus said, *You are the light of the world. A city on a hill cannot be hidden.* [Mat.5:14]

Consider Mary, when the Resurrected Jesus appeared to her. What did she do?

Did she walk casually back to her home and continue with her routine duties? No! She ran to the disciples and said, "He's risen! He's risen! He's risen!" Jesus Himself had reignited her inspiration. She was excited.

Since that resurrection morning followers of Christ have been running to the ends of the earth, shouting, "He's risen!" This is what our family has been doing untiringly for more than 60 years. What sparks our enthusiasm? The life-giving Spirit of Jesus Christ.

And if the Spirit of him who raised Jesus from the dead is living in you, he who raised Christ from the dead will also give life to your mortal bodies because of his Spirit who lives in you. Rom.8:11

Christ even gives divine inspiration for doing life's mundane tasks with a sense of joy. The life of Jesus is why inspired, redeemed believers get up each morning to face a new day with purpose.

May our Lord Jesus Christ himself and God our Father, who loved us and by his grace gave us eternal encouragement and good hope, encourage your hearts and strengthen you in every good deed and word.[2Th.2:16-17]

❖❖❖

YOU DON'T HAVE to live a bored life one more day. **Be inspired! GIVE THANKS! Spend time in the presence of Jesus. Allow His Spirit to fill you. You will begin to live excited because** *your inspiration is reignited.*

❖❖❖

N – NATURE REBORN

It is easy to GIVE THANKS because of the miracle that is ours through Jesus.

> — *Our nature is reborn* —
> because of Christ's
> great sacrifice on our behalf.

Through these [His glory and goodness] *he has given us his very great and precious promises, so that through them* **you may participate in** [be partakers of] **the divine nature**, *having escaped the corruption in the world caused by evil desires* (emphasis added).[2Pet.1:4]

1. We are no longer the old persons that we were before Christ redeemed us.

2. When we accepted Christ, *God's nature in us was reborn.*

> # Humanity's original, created nature was the nature of God.

From the beginning, God intended for His human creation to have His nature.

Then God said, "Let us make human beings in our image, in our likeness, so that they may rule over the fish in the sea and the birds in the sky, over the livestock and all the wild animals, and over all the creatures that move along the ground." So God created human beings in his own image, in the image of God he created them; male and female he created them. Gen.1:26-27

The enemy, referred to in Genesis as the serpent, came into the Garden of Eden and cunningly caused Adam and Eve to turn away from God. (Genesis 3) The moment that they doubted God's integrity, the beautiful relationship between God and His human creation was broken. When that relationship was fractured, Adam and Eve no longer possessed the nature of God. They became slaves of Satan (the serpent) and became partakers of his character. Sin and death became the essential nature of all humankind. (Read my book, GOD'S BIG PICTURE to understand God's plan for people and to find yourself in His eternal plan.)

When Christ came, as God's offering for our sin, He did all that was necessary to restore humanity back to God's original purpose, to be the expressions of His image, His life and His nature in this physical world.

Many born again Christians have never understood that when they accepted Christ, they received a new nature, God's divine life.

Through these [His glory and goodness] *he has given us his very great and precious promises, so that through them* **you may participate in** [be partakers of] **the divine nature**, *having escaped the corruption in the world caused by evil desires* (emphasis added).[2Pet.1:4]

The nature of God is reborn in you.

That is fact. Your nature is no longer critical, vindictive, jealous, angry, insecure, bitter, or vengeful. Your nature is now love. You do not have to struggle, trying to have God's nature. This is part of the miracle that takes place when you are born again. All you must do is believe that you have Christ's life and nature and then cooperate with the Holy Spirit who causes the divine nature to be expressed through you.

Are you living according to this divine nature? You can choose to benefit from His presence and His nature in every area of your life.

For example, when things happen that you do not like, you can choose whether to react according to your old nature (out of habit) or to respond according to your new nature.

Ungodly emotions no longer have the power to rule your life. Choose to allow the nature of God to be expressed through you in every situation. You can do it, by the power of Christ's Spirit at work in you.

For in Christ all the fullness of the Deity lives in bodily form, and in Christ you have been brought to fullness. He is the head over every power and authority. Col.2:9-10

for it is God who works in you to will and to act in order to fulfill his good purpose. Phil.2:13

The Spirit-filled believer both has the nature of God and has the power to live according to that new divine status.

Believe that you have the discipline to live according to God's life and nature in you.

✧✧✧

LET US REMIND ourselves that:

We have been given exceedingly great and precious promises that provide to us all that Christ has accomplished through His action of redemption on our behalf.

We are now partakers of God's divine nature.

We are delivered from our old sinful nature.

We accept God's new life by faith in the redeeming work of Jesus Christ.

We GIVE THANKS to our Redeemer, because *our nature is reborn*.

✧✧✧

G – GOSPEL REVEALED

As we GIVE THANKS to God, we remember that through Christ and His work of redemption on our behalf:

— The Gospel has been revealed. —

During my global ministry travels, I encounter many people, including Christians and even pastors, who do not have a full understanding of the gospel. They have not discovered the empowering biblical truths that enable believers to live according to their new redeemed status. Often, Christians have not comprehended that the righteousness that comes from God is revealed in the gospel.

For in the gospel the righteousness of God is revealed — a righteousness that is by faith from first to last, just as it is written: "The righteous will live by faith."[Rom.1:17]

The gospel includes four fundamental truths:

1. God created humankind — male and female — in His own image;

2. Through deception, the enemy of God became the ruler over God's beautiful human creation, but God promised that a Redeemer would come;

3. God came in Christ Jesus to redeem humankind — through His own life-sacrifice — and to restore to humanity God's original purpose; and

4. Everyone who accepts Christ's death on the cross and His victorious resurrection as being for them personally is restored to relationship with God as He intended from the beginning.

In each of these fundamental gospel

truths, the goodness of God is revealed; His righteousness bestowed on people is shown.

God made him (Christ) who had no sin to be sin for us, so that in him we might become the righteousness of God. 2Cor.5:21

The gospel is revealed in Jesus Christ. We must allow Him to become Lord:

1. To become the center of every occasion;
2. To be the principal character in our lives;
3. To be our truth and reality; and
4. To be the divine presence that we depend upon.

The gospel points to Jesus.

Just as the gospel focuses our attention on Jesus, as the Source of life, so He directs our attention to the power and urgency of the gospel. The gospel is more than a message; it is a revelation of God through Jesus Christ.

Jesus calls each of us to reveal His gospel to others so that they can know Him too.

...go into all the world and preach the gospel... Mk.16:15 NKJV

The Apostle Paul understood this priority and the profound power within the gospel.

I am not ashamed of the gospel, because it is the power of God that brings salvation to everyone who believes: first to the Jew, then to the Gentile. Rom.1:16

- The gospel is centered in Jesus Christ.

- The gospel is the power of God.

- The gospel is for everyone.

- The gospel must be believed.
- The gospel brings salvation.
- The gospel brings to us God's own righteousness.
- The gospel shows to us the amazing goodness of God.

I am grateful for the gospel.

I am thankful for Jesus.

Through Jesus we have everything that is good, that is divine, that is fulfilling, that restores wholeness to every area of our lives.

This is Salvation!

Salvation is found in no one else, for there is no other name given under heaven by which we must be saved…[Ac.4:12]

There is no other *name* that has eternal power.

There is no other *power* that conquers all.

There is no other *solution* to the human problem.

Jesus is our **yesterday** — our past sins are remitted. ..."*For I will forgive their wickedness and will remember their sins no more.*"Jer.31:34

Jesus is our **today** — He announced: ...*I am the way and the truth and the life...*Jn.14:6

He is our **tomorrow** — He says: ..."*Never will I leave you; never will I forsake you.*"Heb.13:5.

*Jesus Christ is the same yesterday and today and forever.*Heb.13:8

- Jesus is the Tower that we look to.

- Jesus is the Wall of Protection that shields us.

- Jesus is the Provider who dispenses the grain in the marketplace of our needs.

- Jesus is the Water of Life that pours into us and renews us daily.

- Jesus is the Captain of the Lord's army.

- Jesus is the eternally Victorious One.

- Jesus is the one who makes a way where there is no way.

- Jesus is the presence that blooms in our desert.

- Jesus is the Father to the fatherless.

- Jesus is the husband to the widow.

- Jesus is the provider of eternal life.

- Jesus is the giver of a new kind of peace.

- Jesus is the name above every name.

- Jesus is our Healer.

JESUS IS EVERYTHING!

Whoever has the Son has life… 1Jn.5:12

✧✧✧

AS WE LIVE our lives day-to-day we can be confident that we are not alone; that we have a connection; that we have a purpose; that we have been reclaimed; and that we have a future and a hope.

We can overcome any problem that arises and GIVE THANKS because *the gospel of Christ has been revealed* to us, in us and through us.

Chapter 2

–Giving Thanks–
A Way of Life

SO OFTEN WE relate the term *thanksgiving* with family dinners or special events to honor the faithfulness of God. But thanksgiving is much more than one special day in the year.

> **Giving thanks is a way of life**
> **–it is part of every day!**

Purpose to GIVE THANKS to the Lord for His mercy, which lasts forever. (Psalms 100:5 NKJV)

Remember the great work of redemption that has been accomplished by Jesus Christ and GIVE THANKS.

✧✧✧

T – Transgressions Remitted

*your transgressions
your sins are removed*

Jesus' blood was shed for the remission of sin.

Mat.26:28

H – Health Renewed

your health is renewed

You have been healed by the stripes and wounds of Jesus.

Isa.53:5

A – Authority Regained

you have authority

As a believer you have been entrusted with authority.

Mat.16:19

N – Name Recorded

*your name is recorded in
the Lamb's book of life*

Christ's sacrifice for you made it possible for your name to be recorded in His Book of Life.

Rev.21:27

K – Kinship Restored

*your kinship relationship
with God is restored*

To everyone who has received Jesus Christ, He has given them the right to be His kinfolk, His children, the relatives of His family.

Jn.1:12

S – Song Returned

your song has been returned

Since Jesus saved you, you are able to sing a new song to Him. A song of praise and gratitude, a song of resurrection.

Psa.40:3

G – Guilt Removed

all guilt is removed from your life by God

As a believer you can choose to resist the feelings of guilt, by re-membering the grace of God that provided your great salvation.

Rom.8:1; 2Cor.5:21

I – Inferiority Replaced

***your inferiority is replaced
with godly dignity.***

Jesus stood up in the midst of
your disgrace and said, "You are
chosen. You are special. You are
redeemed."

1Pet.2:9 NKJV; Jn.15:16

V – Value Restated

your value is restated

Your worth was determined by
God Himself. Jesus' blood was
the most valuable gift of all time.
Christ came and restated the
eternal fact of your value.

1Pet.1:18-19; 1Jn.3:1

I – Inspiration Reignited

*you are brought into a life
of light and inspiration*

Jesus is the one who ignites His inspiration deep within you. He rescues you and energizes you.

Rom.15:13

N – Nature Reborn

your nature is reborn

From the beginning, God intended for His human creation to have His nature. When you accepted Christ, you received His divine nature.

2Pet.1:4

G – Gospel Revealed

The Gospel has been revealed.

The gospel points to Jesus. Through Jesus Christ and His work of redemption on your behalf the gospel is revealed. The gospel of Christ is now revealed to you, in you and through you.

2Cor.5:21; Rom.1:16-17

Friend, based on Christ's redemption you can live each day in awe of your Savior's amazing love. Take time to remember what He has done for you. Express appreciation with the spirit of gratitude and GIVE THANKS.

✧✧✧

If you have not yet embraced Jesus as a living reality in your life, do it now as you pray this prayer. If you will believe that Jesus suffered for you personally, and accept that His sacrifice was adequate to provide Salvation and a new life, you will be saved.

Right now, PRAY TO THE LORD right out loud.

O Lord in heaven:

I do, here and now, believe that you came to earth as Jesus Christ. I believe that in Your great mercy and love, You died for me, as my personal substitute.

I believe that You suffered all of the penalty of my sins and that You paid the full price so that there is no more debt for sin that I must pay.

Thank you for your love for me. Thank you for taking my place and for paying what was owed for all of my sins.

Now I am now redeemed. I am saved.

I believe on You, Lord Jesus. I

believe that you are alive and that you come to live in me.

I welcome You into my heart as my Savior from sin and hell, and from all the power of the devil.

I accept You, Jesus, as Lord of my life. I have come to You with all my heart, as a helpless, guilty sinner, seeking salvation, and trusting only in Your sacrifice on my behalf.

Thank You, Lord, for my full salvation.

I am redeemed. My sins are forgiven. I am saved. I believe on Jesus Christ. I am a Christian—a follower of Jesus Christ, the Son of God.

From this moment, I will strive to follow You and to share your Good News with others so that they can receive Your life too.

Amen.

✧✧✧

If you believe the Bible promises contained in this book and if you have sincerely prayed and received Jesus into your life by faith, then your sins are forgiven.[Col.1:14] An angel is recording your name *in the Lamb's book of life,*[Rev.21:27] right now. Only believe. Jesus lives in you now.[Gal.2:20] You have His life.[1Jn.5:12]

Since your sins are now *purged,*[Heb.1:3] they can no longer condemn you.

Confess with faith that Christ's redemption is yours today.

Remember that your sins have been forgiven.

Declare that your sicknesses have been carried away.

Believe that every provision of Christ's work of redemption is for you and begin to GIVE THANKS.

❖❖❖

AS AN ACT of faith and gratefulness, register your commitment on the next page. It will be a lasting testimony of your personal experience today. Be definite about it. Being thankful is a lifestyle that demonstrates that you and Jesus are now friends.

MY COMMITMENT

Today I have read this book, GIVE THANKS. I am a redeemed child of God, therefore I have many reasons to be thankful.

I have received new insight concerning my relationship with God through Jesus Christ. Today I make a commitment to express my thanks to God every day. I commit my life to do my best to please Him in all that I think and say and do. With His grace and help, I will remember all that Christ's redeeming work has provided to me and I will share Jesus with others.

Depending on Him to keep me by His grace, I have made this commitment today — in Jesus' name.

Signature: _____

Date: _____

If your enemy, the devil, ever tries to make you doubt what has taken place, or tries to cause you to be ungrateful, refer to this commitment that you have made today. Reflect on the reasons that you have to GIVE THANKS.

Live each day with an attitude of thanksgiving.

Give thanks to the LORD, for he is good; his love endures forever. 1Chr.16:34

We are earnestly praying for God's best to come to you and your loved ones. Stay in touch with us; we enjoy hearing from you. Your commitment to be thankful is the beginning of a lifestyle of gratitude that pleases the Lord.

There are many ministry resources available on our *osborn.org* website to help you grow in your faith and to help you experience all that Christ has made available to you.

GIVE THANKS

I encourage you to study the Redemption Lessons that are available to you on our website. Knowing these truths produces God's best in your life.

✳

"**W**e have one message – Jesus Christ and His ministry to forgive, heal and restore people to fellowship with God. Everyone is included in this GOOD NEWS message of what is available through Christ's redemptive work for humankind."

– LaDonna C. Osborn

When Dr. T.L. saw Jesus alive in a vision in 1948, the ministries of T.L. & Daisy and their entire family – for generations to come – were forever changed. The healing power of Christ and His resurrection LIFE is the Osborns' central message.

Raised on the platforms of global miracle evangelism, Osborn daughter Dr. LaDonna's worldwide ministry is also marked by supernatural healing miracles. Why? Because Jesus and His ministry are the same TODAY as in Bible days.

Before each public evangelism Festival of Faith and Miracles, Dr. Osborn teaches the truths of Christ and His divine plan to pastors and Christian believers during her Gospel Seminars.

The people are eager to learn. Their notebooks are being filled with words that convey the profound truths of God's plan for His people. It is biblical TRUTH that will make the difference in the lives and ministries of these Christian workers.

Osborn Gospel Festivals worldwide

AFRICA

INDIA

ASIA

T.L. and LaDonna are committed to Christ's ministry. What He began during His earthly life, is to be continued by His followers. The Osborns are agents of Christ's healing LIFE to the ends of the earth.

The Osborns' arsenal of Gospel books and teaching courses are impacting people in practically every nation on earth. TONS of these Christ-centered materials have been distributed to soulwinners, Bible School students and searchers for truth. Books in new languages are being added each year.

Osborn Book Distributions worldwide

INDIA

ASIA

AFRICA

After the multitude of men, women, youth and children receive Christ as Savior at the Festivals of Faith and Healing, Dr. Osborn prepares them to receive their healing. She teaches them the promises of God which are her authority as she commands the spirits of disease to leave the people.

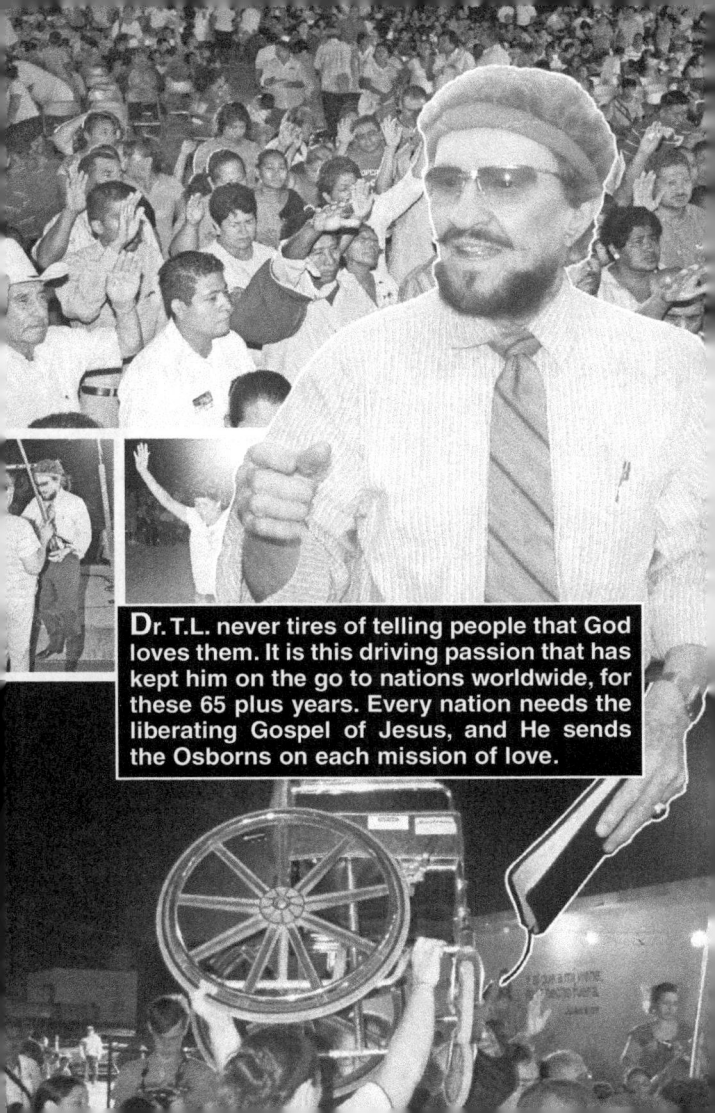

Dr. T.L. never tires of telling people that God loves them. It is this driving passion that has kept him on the go to nations worldwide, for these 65 plus years. Every nation needs the liberating Gospel of Jesus, and He sends the Osborns on each mission of love.

LaDonna C. Osborn Festival

Kikwit, Democratic Republic of the Congo

of Faith and Miracles worldwide

Tens of thousands of weary Congolese gather to hear a message of hope from Dr. LaDonna. Thousands believe on and accept Jesus Christ after hearing the Gospel. Marvelous miracles of healing are witnessed daily.

Dr. LaDonna Osborn is experiencing BIBLE DAYS in Point-Noire, Congo. *The blind receive their sight, and the lame walk ... the deaf hear ... and the poor have the Gospel preached to them.* Mat 11:5

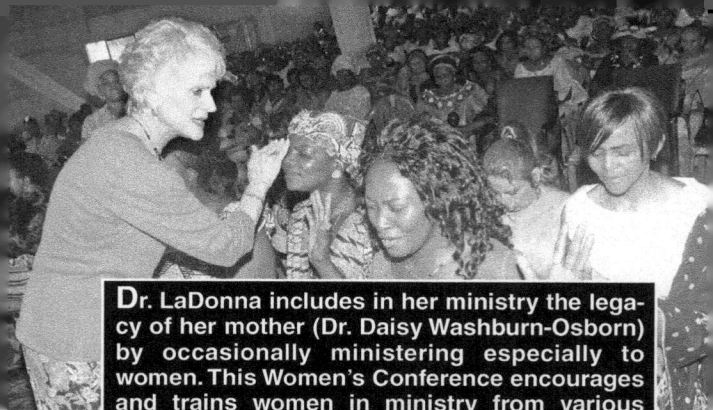

Dr. LaDonna includes in her ministry the legacy of her mother (Dr. Daisy Washburn-Osborn) by occasionally ministering especially to women. This Women's Conference encourages and trains women in ministry from various nations of the world.

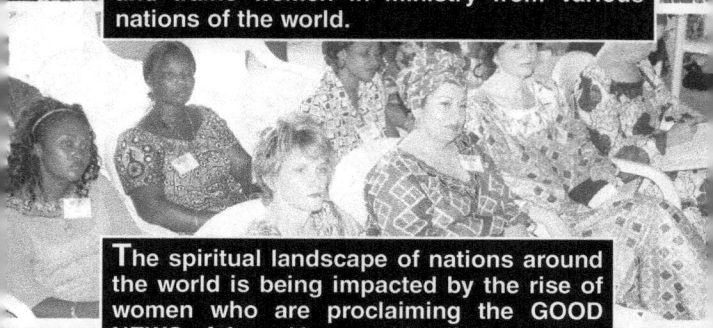

The spiritual landscape of nations around the world is being impacted by the rise of women who are proclaiming the GOOD NEWS of Jesus' love and healing power.

The Osborns generally pray for people *en mass*. There are no limits with God. If He can heal one, He can also heal thousands at the same time. However, when possible they love to lay their hands on individual persons and pray.

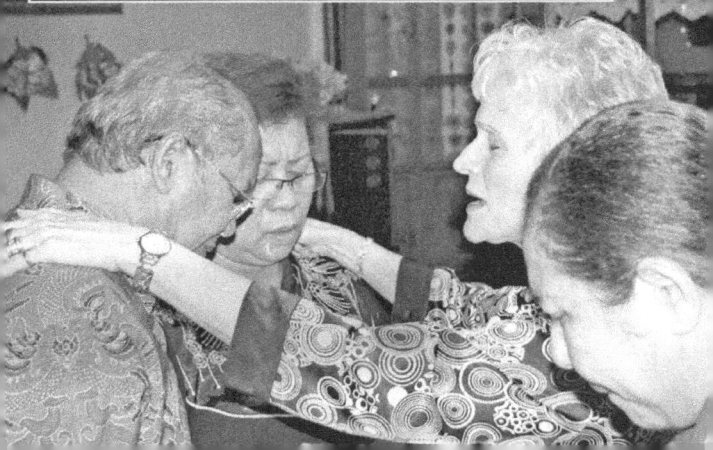

OSBORN MINISTRIES –

- Angola
- Argentina
- Armenia
- Australia
- Austria
- Azerbaijan
- Bangladesh
- Belarus
- Belgium
- Benin
- Bermuda
- Bolivia
- Botswana
- Brazil
- Bulgaria
- Burkina Faso
- Burundi

- Cambodia
- Cameroon
- Canada
- Central Afr. Rep.
- Chad
- Chile
- China
- Colombia
- Congo (Dem. Rep.)
- Congo (Rep.)
- Costa Rica
- Cuba
- Denmark
- Dominican Rep.
- Ecuador
- Egypt
- El Salvador
- England
- Estonia
- Ethiopia
- Finland
- France
- Gabon

- Georgia
- Germany
- Ghana
- Guatemala
- Haiti
- Honduras

LEGEND

Nations in which the Osborns have proclaimed the Gospel in face-to-face ministry.

And he said unto them, Go ye into all the wo

OVER 60 YEARS – OVER 100 NATIONS

- Hong Kong
- India
- Indonesia
- Ireland
- Italy
- Ivory Coast
- Jamaica
- Japan
- Kazakhstan
- Kenya
- Kyrgyzstan
- Laos
- Liberia
- Lithuania
- Luxemborg
- Madagascar
- Malawi
- Malaysia
- Mexico
- Mongolia
- Myanmar
- Netherlands

- New Zealand
- Nicaragua
- Nigeria
- Norway
- Pakistan
- Panama
- Papua N.Guinea
- Paraguay
- Peru
- Philippines
- Poland
- Portugal
- Puerto Rico
- Russia

- Rwanda
- Senegal
- South Africa
- South Korea
- Spain
- Sri Lanka
- Sweden
- Switzerland
- Taiwan
- Tajikistan
- Tanzania
- Thailand
- Togo
- Trinidad
- Uganda
- Ukraine
- United States
- Uruguay
- Uzbekistan
- Venezuela
- Vietnam
- Virgin Islands
- Zambia

*nd preach the gospel to every creature.*Mk.16:15

Christ's Ministry of Healing Continues Today...

Dr. LaDonna C. Osborn   Dr. T.L. Osborn

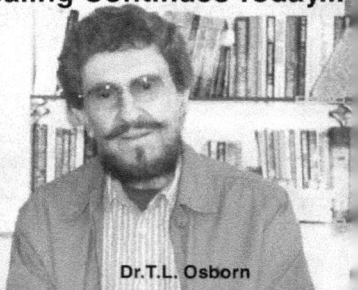

...through PUBLIC MIRACLE EVENTS in over 100 countries

...through GOSPEL MATERIALS in over 130 languages worldwide

...through teaching the promises of God in PUBLIC SEMINARS

...through EQUIPPING BELIEVERS WORLDWIDE for evangelism

...through PRAYER & INTERCESSION for Partners & the World

"**P**artnership in this global ministry is miraculous. As we GO and REACH and LIFT and TOUCH people in Christ's name, you – our Partner – GO WITH US. It is YOUR ministry in action. PARTNERSHIP IS MINISTRY MULTIPLIED!"
– T.L. & LaDonna Osborn

The *MISSION*
Of Christianity

THE GLOBAL MISSION of Christianity is to witness of Christ and of His resurrection to *the entire world—* to *every creature.* (See Mk.16:15)

The Apostle Paul said, ..."*Everyone who calls on the name of the Lord will be saved.*" Rom.10:13

T.L. and Daisy Osborn shared a worldwide ministry together for over five decades, before her demise in 1995. T.L. continues his global ministry to multitudes.

The Osborn daughter, Dr. LaDonna, is the leader of the Osborns' world ministry. She is involved on practically every continent via face-to-face ministry, through public mass evangelism *Festivals of Faith and Miracles*, trans-evangelical *Gospel Seminars*.

As CEO of *OSBORN Ministries International*, Dr. LaDonna's expertise is making possible the expansion of this ministry in nations around the world. Learn more about the Osborn global outreaches through their website at ***osborn.org.***

Drs. T.L., Daisy and LaDonna Osborn have reached millions for Christ in over a hundred nations during more than six decades. This ministry-brief is included here to inspire young believers that they, too, can carry the *gospel torch into all the world.*(See Mk.16:15)

Mass Miracle Evangelism

Tommy Lee Osborn and Daisy Marie Washburn were married in Los Banos, California in 1942, at the ages of 17 and 18. In 1945 they went to India as missionaries but were unable to convince the people of these ancient religions — Muslims and Hindus — about Christ. They had not yet discovered the truths about healing miracles. They returned to the USA dismayed and disheartened — but not dissuaded.

Soon after their demoralizing return home, the Lord appeared to them both, at different times, as they searched for the answer to their dilemma.

- They began to discover the Bible truths that create faith for biblical miracles.

- They had learned in India that for people of non-Christian nations to believe the gospel, they must witness miracle proof that Jesus Christ is alive today.

- They discovered that signs, miracles and wonders are essential to convincing *non*-Christian nations about the gospel.

Jesus was...*accredited by God to you by **miracles, wonders** and **signs**, which God did among you through him, as you yourselves know* (emphasis added).[Ac.2:22]

These dynamic truths created in their spirits fresh faith in God's Word. With this new lease on life and having discovered the scriptural facts about miracles they, along with their children, *re*-launched their soulwinning saga in 1949—this time in the Caribbean island-nation of Jamaica.

During thirteen weeks of ministry there, hundreds of biblical miracles confirmed their preaching.

- Over a hundred deaf-mutes were healed;

- Over ninety totally blind people received sight;

- Hundreds of crippled, paralyzed and lame people were restored;

- Most important of all, *nearly ten thousand souls received Jesus Christ as their Savior.*

That success motivated their new global ministry, proclaiming the gospel to multitudes. In the era when developing nations were mostly *colonized* by European governments, the Osborns pioneered the concept of *Mass Miracle Evangelism.* Such methods had not been witnessed since the epoch of the Early Church. T.L. and Daisy addressed audiences of tens of thousands throughout the dangerous years of *nationalism* when the awakening of many developing nations was repulsing foreign political domination.

Their example inspired national men and women, globally, to arise from their restrictive past, and to become leading gospel messengers and church builders in the unevangelized nations of the world. Many of them are numbered among the most distinguished and successful Christian leaders today.

The largest churches in the world are no longer in America or Europe. Anointed and talented national pastors are raising them up. Single churches in Africa seat 50,000 plus people. To God be the glory.

Drs. T.L. and Daisy's partial testimony is recorded for posterity in their 512 page unique pictorial, THE GOSPEL ACCORDING TO T.L. AND DAISY.

Global Evangelism Concepts

During T.L. and Daisy's unprecedented years as an evangelism team, they inaugurated numerous programs to reach the unreached. Their concept of *National Missionary Assistance* resulted in them sponsoring over 30,000 national preachers as full time missionaries to unevangelized tribes and villages where new, self-supporting churches became established globally.

The Osborn literature is published in more than 130 languages. Their Docu-Miracle crusade films, audio and video CDs and DVDs, and their digital productions (including Bible courses), are produced in over 70 languages and are circulated around the world.

They have provided airlifts and huge shipments of literature and of soulwinning tools for gospel ministries abroad. They have furnished scores of four-wheel drive vehicles equipped with films, projectors, screens, generators, public-address systems, audiocassettes and cassette players, plus literature for reaching the unreached.

Publishing The Gospel

Dr. Daisy's five major books are *pace-setters* in Christian literature for women — *unique examples of **inclusive** language that consistently addresses both men and women.*

Dr. T.L. has authored over 20 major books. He wrote his first, HEALING THE SICK, during their mission to Jamaica in 1950. Now in its 46th edition, it is a global favorite, used as a Bible School text book in many nations.

The publisher calls HEALING THE SICK — *A Living Classic* — a faith-building best seller since 1950. Over a million copies are in print, circulating healing truth throughout the world.

Dr. LaDonna's book, GOD'S BIG PICTURE is published in scores of languages and is heralded globally as the single most important book to make clear the story of the Bible, from Genesis to Revelation. Through this book, people discover their place in God's plan.

Some of her other books, such as CHAOS OF MIRACLES, JESUS IS TOUCHING SOSHANGUVE and UNKNOWN BUT NOT FORGOTTEN are modern day accounts of Christ's ministry in action through her as she ministers the gospel among some of the world's unreached masses.

Their Global Saga

In T.L.'s ninth decade of life, the Osborn Ministries International continues to expand. Following Daisy's demise, T.L. has continued his global evangelism crusades, and his daughter, Dr. LaDonna, has enlarged her ministries of evangelism and training to nearly every continent as she carries the *torch of the gospel* into this century's new frontiers.

Like the Apostle Paul, LaDonna says:

> *I am not ashamed of the gospel, because it is the power of God that brings salvation to everyone who believes...*
> Rom.1:16

She believes that:

*The World is the **Heart** of the Church,*
*The Church is the **Hope** of the World.*

She contends that:

Without the *World*, the *Church is **meaningless** —*
Without the *Church*, the *World is **hopeless**.*

Colonialism
Nationalism
Globalism/Evangelism

Dr. LaDonna Osborn knows the ministry of World Evangelism. Since childhood, she has lived on the front lines of global SOULWINNING — from the days of *colonialism,* through the turbulent years of *nationalism,* and into this century of *globalism, mass evangelism* and *national* and *international Church growth.*

The Osborns hold forth these simple truths:

1. That the Bible is as valid today as it ever was;

2. That the divine calling for every believer is to witness of Christ to the unconverted;

3. That every soul won to Christ can become His representative; and

4. That miracles, signs and wonders are what distinguish Christianity from being just another philosophical religion.

To demonstrate these biblical issues is the essence of the global *MISSION of Christianity.*

Just as with the Apostle Paul, Dr. LaDonna and Dr. T.L. state:

> *...the task the Lord Jesus has given me — the task of testifying to the good news of God's grace.*[Ac.20:24] *...we can preach the gospel in the regions beyond...*[2Cor.10:16]

The history of the Osborn Ministries International is also recorded in their unique and historical 24-volume *Encyclo-Biographical Anthology*. It contains more than 23,000 pages, 30,946 photos, 636 *Faith Digest* magazines, 2,024 pages of personal, hand-written diary notes, 1,011 pages of Osborns' news letters, 1,062 pages of unpublished historical data about their world ministry, 2,516 world mission reports, and 6,113 Christian ministry reports.

These 24 giant tomes span over six feet of shelf space and have taken their place in the archives and libraries of institutions of higher learning around the world, including such renowned uni-

versities and libraries as: University of
Cambridge, Cambridge, England; University
of Oxford, Oxford, England;
Asbury Theological Seminary, Wilmore,
USA; British Library, London, England;
Central Bible College, Springfield, USA;
Christ for the Nations, Dallas, USA;
Fuller Theological Seminary, Pasadena,
USA; Messenger College, Joplin, USA;
National Library, Sofia, Bulgaria; Oral
Roberts University, Tulsa, USA; Ramkhamhaeng
University, Bangkok, Thailand;
Regent University, Virginia Beach,
USA; Universidad Interamericana de
Puerto Rico, Ponce, Puerto Rico; Université
de Cocody, Abidjan, Ivory Coast;
University of Ghana, Legon-Accra, Ghana;
Université de Kinshasa, Kinshasa, Democratic
Republic of the Congo; Université
de Lomé, Lomé, Togo; University of
Nairobi, Nairobi, Kenya; University of
Maseno, Maseno, Kenya; Université
Marien Ngouabi, Brazzaville, Congo;

Université Omar Bongo, Libreville, Gabon; University of Wales, Bangor, Wales; Vernadsky National Library, Kiev, Ukraine; Word of Life, Uppsala, Sweden; (plus many more), and the archives of many leading denominational headquarters.

✧✧✧

- The Osborns' continuing passion:

  *To express and propagate
  the gospel of Jesus Christ
  to all people throughout
  the world.*

- Their tenet for action:

  *No one deserves to hear the
  gospel repeatedly before
  everyone has heard it at
  least once.*

- Their motto:

  *One Way—Jesus;
  One Job—Evangelism.*

- Their guiding principle:

  *Every Christian believer—
  a witness for Christ.*

The witness is expressed best by the words of the Apostle John:

who testifies to everything he saw — that is, the word of God and the testimony of Jesus Christ.[Rev.1:2] We testify *...of these things, and wrote these things; and we know that* (our) *...testimony is true* (emphasis added).[Jn. 21:24 NKJV]

✳

BOOKS BY THE OSBORNS

BELIEVERS IN ACTION—*Apostolic–Rejuvenating*

BIBLICAL HEALING—*Seven Miracle Keys*
4 Visions–60+ yrs. of Proof

CHAOS OF MIRACLES
Christ's Historic & Supernatural Visitation to the DRC

FIVE CHOICES FOR WOMEN WHO WIN
21st Century Options

GIVE THANKS—*Reflections on Christ's Redemption*

GOD'S BIG PICTURE—*An Impelling Gospel Classic*

GOD'S LIFE IN YOU—*52 Facts*
Discover God's Purpose in You

GOD'S LOVE PLAN—*The Awesome Discovery*

HEALING THE SICK—*A Living Classic*

JESUS & WOMEN—*Big Questions Answered*

JESUS IS TOUCHING SOSHANGUVE
God's Love Revealed in South Africa

LIFE–TRIUMPH OVER TRAGEDY (WHY)
A True Story of Life After Death

MIRACLES-PROOF of God's Love

NEW LIFE FOR WOMEN—*Reality Refocused*

NEW MIRACLE LIFE NOW—*For Asia and The World*
A Global Communiqué of The Christian Faith

OUR WITNESS—*Proof of the Resurrection*

PEACE IS A LIFESTYLE—*Truths for Crisis Times*

SOULWINNING—*Outside The Sanctuary*
A Classic on Biblical Christianity & Human Dignity

THE BEST OF LIFE—*Seven Energizing Dynamics*

THE GOOD LIFE—*A Mini-Bible School–1,519 Ref.*

THE GOSPEL ACCORDING TO T.L. & DAISY
Their Life & World Ministry–510 pg. Pictorial

THE MESSAGE THAT WORKS
T.L.'s Revealing Manifesto on Biblical Faith

THE POWER OF POSITIVE DESIRE
An Invigorating Faith Perspective

THE WOMAN BELIEVER
Awareness of God's Design

UNKNOWN BUT NOT FORGOTTEN
The Gospel Reaches Parakou, Benin

WOMAN WITHOUT LIMITS
Unmuzzled—Unfettered—Unimpeded

WOMEN & SELF-ESTEEM
Divine Royalty Unrestrained

YOU ARE GOD'S BEST
Transforming Life Discoveries

GLOBAL PUBLISHER

OSBORN INTERNATIONAL
P.O. Box 10
Tulsa, OK 74102 USA

❖❖❖

FRENCH DISTRIBUTOR

POSITIVE CONNEXION
BP 2072
51073 Reims Cedex, France

❖❖❖

GERMAN PUBLISHER

SHALOM — VERLAG
Pachlinger Strrasse 10
D-93486 Runding, CHAM, Germany

❖❖❖

PORTUGUESE PUBLISHER

GRACA EDITORIAL
Caixa Postal 1815
Rio de Janiero–RJ–20001, Brazil

❖❖❖

SPANISH PUBLISHER

LIBROS DESAFIO, Apdo. 29724
Bogota, Colombia

_____

(For Quantity Orders, Request Discount Prices.)

WWW.OSBORN.ORG